D1708974

THE BRIGHT LIGHT

AND THE SUPER SCARY DARKNESS

To Josiah,
my sweet boy
with smiling
eyes.

ISBN: 978-1-0877-0935-2
Published by B&H Publishing Group, Nashville, Tennessee

DEWEY: C152.4
SUBHD: FEAR / COURAGE / FEAR IN CHILDREN
Printed in Dongguan, Guangdong, China, in June 2020
1 2 3 4 5 • 24 23 22 21 20

THE BRIGHT LIGHT AND THE SUPER SCARY DARKNESS

Dan DeWitt

illustrations by Rea Zhai

Have you ever been afraid of the dark?

I know I have.

Sometimes the darkness can be super scary.

Sleeping

Screeeeeek.

Smorggggg.

Splurrrttt.

Things make
weird noises
in the dark.

Did you know the Bible
talks a lot about light
and darkness?

In fact, the whole Bible is really one big story about the light and the dark.

At the beginning of the world,
God said, "Let there be light."
The light shined brightly.

Then God made the very
first people, Adam and Eve,
to walk in the light. They loved
God, and they loved the light.

But one day, Adam and Eve disobeyed God. The Bible calls that sin. The darkness of sin filled the whole world. And the darkness was super scary.

Screeeeek.

Smorggggg.

Splurrrttt.

Before long, people began to love the darkness more than the light. Can you believe that?

The world got darker and darker and darker with every passing day.

Screeeeeek.

Smorggggg.

Splurrrttt.

Sometimes it seemed like the darkness was going to win.

But God still loved the world and the people He made. God promised that one day a baby boy would come into the world. He would be the bright light that defeats the super scary darkness.

The prophets pointed to Him.
The poets sang about Him.
The people couldn't wait to meet Him.

But after years and years, the light still hadn't come into the world. God stopped giving messages of light. The people waited and waited, and the darkness grew and grew.

It seemed like the darkness was definitely winning.

Screeeeek.

Smorggggg.

Splurrrttt.

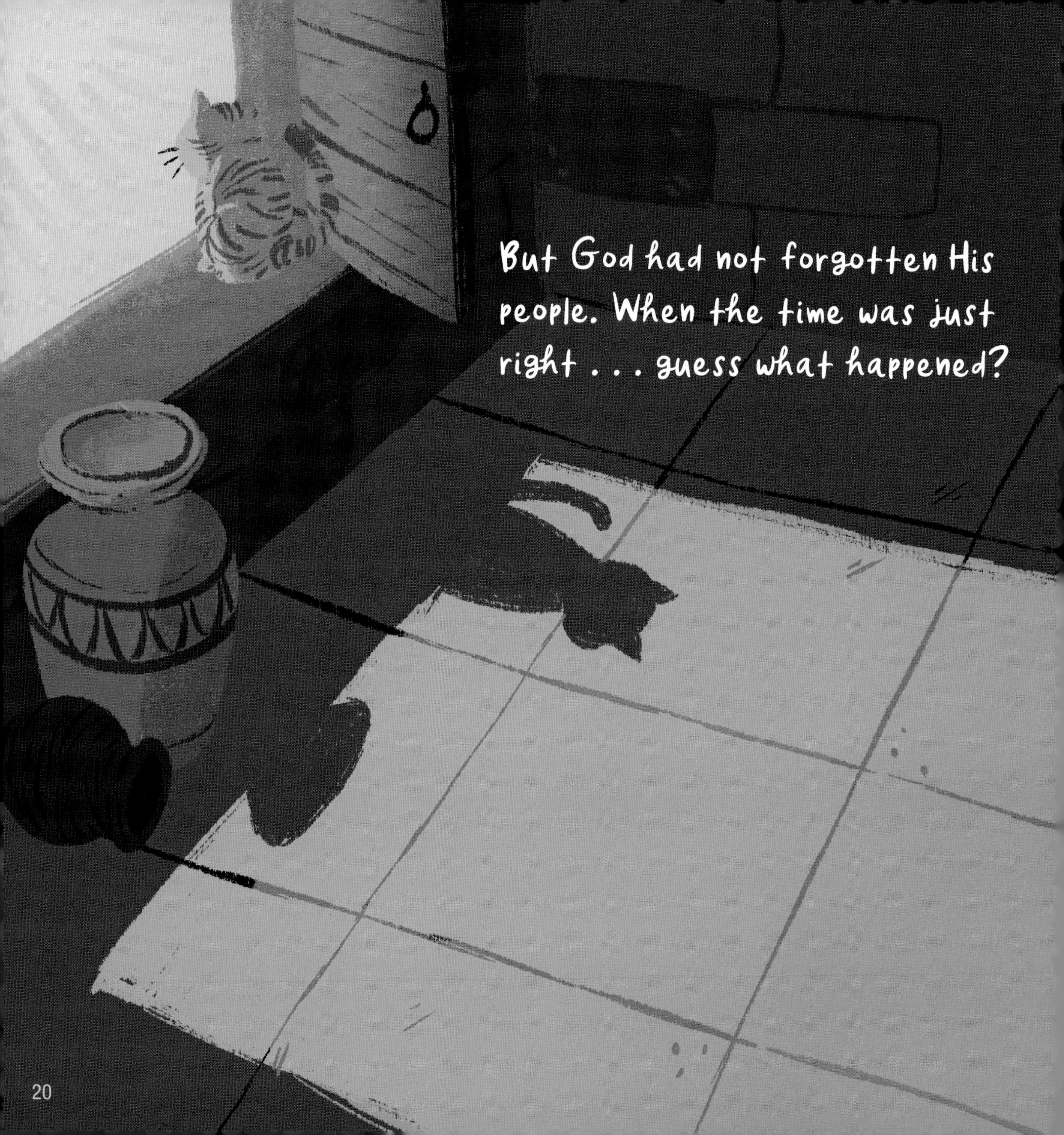

But God had not forgotten His people. When the time was just right . . . guess what happened?

Screeeeeek.
Smorggggg.
Splurrrttt.

God sent the child of light! The chosen, promised baby boy was born. His name was Jesus.

Angels filled the sky, singing songs about the birth of the bright light that defeats the super scary darkness.

When Jesus grew up, He told everyone that He had come to defeat the darkness and bring people true joy.

Screeeeeek.

Smorggggg.

Splurrrttt.

But many people still loved the darkness more than the bright light. And the world grew even darker.

Soon the people were tired of hearing Jesus talk about the light. Sadly, they put Him on a cross to make Him stop.

Jesus died, and the people buried Him in a tomb. It seemed like the darkness had won.

And the super scary darkness grew bigger and darker than ever before.

Screeeeeek.

Smorggggg.

Splurrrttt.

But let me tell you a secret:
the darkness is afraid of the light.
The darkness isn't super scary.
The darkness is a scaredy-cat!

Screeeeeek.

Smorggggg.

Splurrrttt.

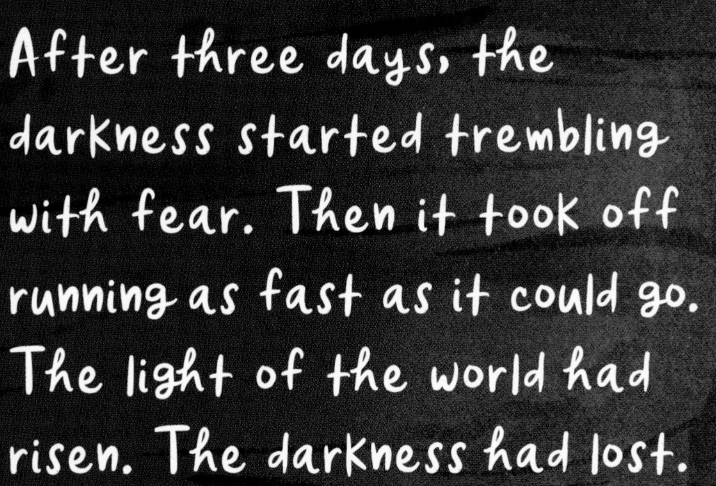

After three days, the darkness started trembling with fear. Then it took off running as fast as it could go. The light of the world had risen. The darkness had lost.

Jesus was alive!

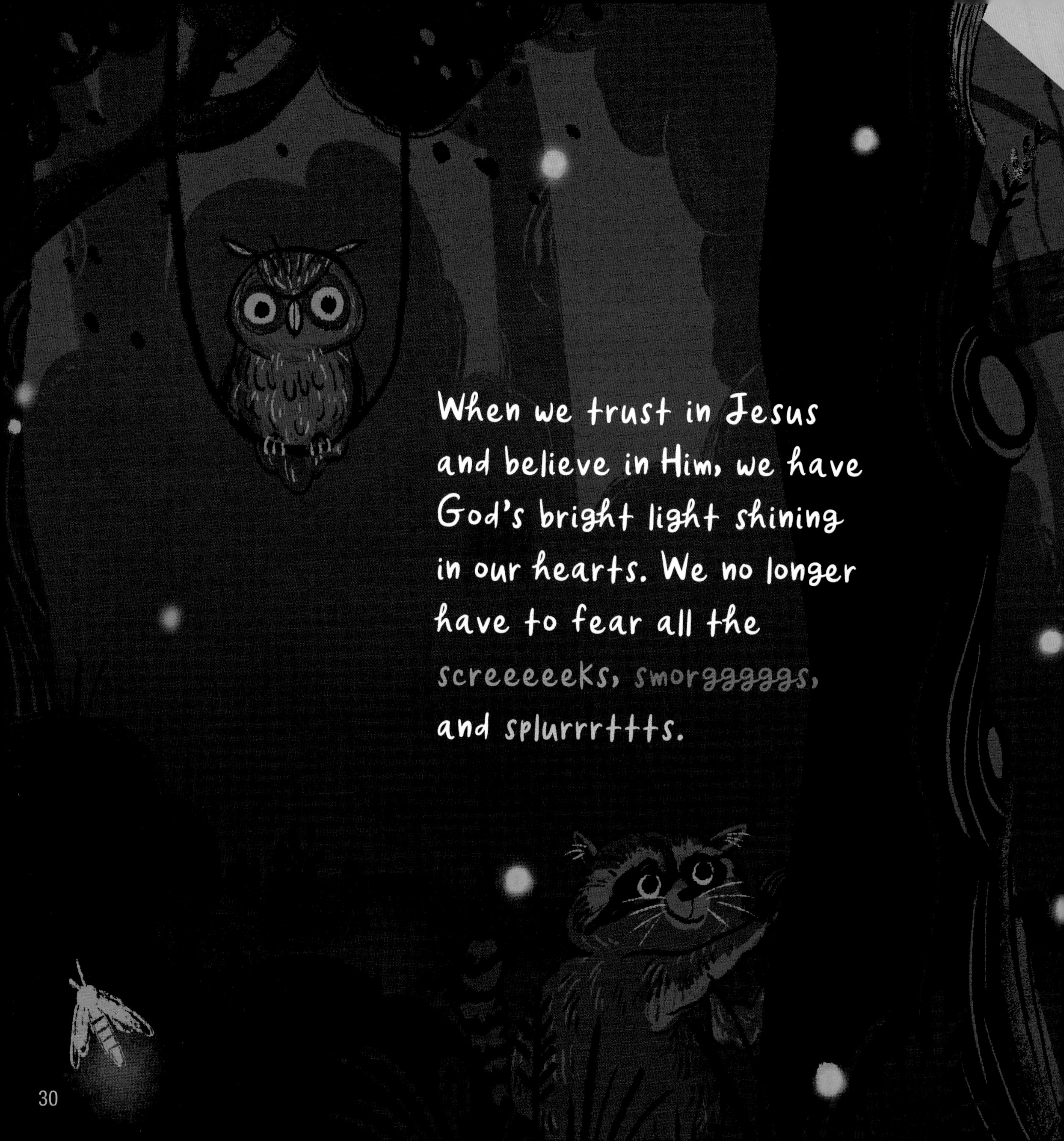

When we trust in Jesus and believe in Him, we have God's bright light shining in our hearts. We no longer have to fear all the screeeeeeks, smorgggggs, and splurrrttts.

Jesus is the bright light that defeats the scaredy-cat darkness!

Remember:

For God, who said, "Light shall shine out of darkness," is the One who has shone in our hearts. —2 Corinthians 4:6 NASB

Read:

John 1:1-5. Jesus called Himself "the light of the world" (John 8:12). What does this mean? This world is dark and scary at times. Yet Jesus' resurrection proves that sin and death have no power over Him (Romans 6:9-10). This is why Jesus is the light of the world, and this is very good news for us! All who trust in Jesus have His bright light inside of us. Darkness no longer has control over us (Colossians 1:13), and darkness does not win (John 1:5).

So, when you are afraid, talk to Jesus. Ask Him for help, calm, and peace. And remember that the darkness you see and feel is not stronger than the light. The darkness is just a scaredy-cat!

Think:

1. What are some super scary things you can think of? Why do you think they are super scary?
2. What can you do when you are afraid? Whom can you talk to? What might you say to Jesus?
3. Have you ever asked Jesus to forgive you for your sins? Have you asked Him to shine His light into your heart and trusted Him with your life?